GOOD MORNING SUNSHINE

GENERAL EDITOR

JACK BOOTH

DAVID BOOTH

WILLA PAULI & JO PHENIX

IMPRESSIONS

HOLT, RINEHART AND WINSTON OF CANADA
a division of
Harcourt Brace & Company Canada, Ltd.
Toronto, Orlando, San Diego, London, Sydney

Cover Illustrator: Heather Cooper

ISBN 0-03-921405-2

Copyright© 1984 Holt, Rinehart and Winston of Canada. A Division of Harcourt Brace & Company Canada, Ltd.
All rights reserved.

Canadian Cataloguing in Publication Data

Main entry under title:
Good Morning Sunshine

(Impressions)
For use in schools.
ISBN 0-03-921405-2

1. Readers (Primary). 2. Readers–1950–
I. Booth, Jack   II. Series.

PE1119.U6   428.6   C83-098248-5

Illustrations and Photographs
Arnold Lobel: pp. 4-10; *Jock Macrae*: pp. 11-13, 41, 88-91, 105-110; *Vesna Krysanovich*: pp. 14-15, 111; *San Murata*: pp. 16-17; *Ilze Bertuss*: p. 18; *Bill Kimber*: pp. 19-31; *John Burningham*: pp. 32-40; *Martin Springett*: pp. 42-45; *Mary Young and Greg Duffel*: pp. 46-52; *Vladyana Krykorka*: pp. 53, 54-55, 64; *Peter Kovalik*: pp. 56-63; *Tana Hoban*: pp. 65-73; *Joanne Fitzgerald*: p. 74; *David Partington*: pp. 75-81; *Barb Reid*: pp. 82-87; *Frank Hammond*: pp. 92-101; *Barbara Klunder*: pp. 102-103; *Lois Lesynski*: p. 104; *Maurice Sendak*: p. 112.

The authors and publishers gratefully acknowledge the consultants listed below for their contribution to the development of this program:

Isobel Bryan   *Primary Consultant   Ottawa Board of Education*
Ethel Buchanan   *Language Arts Consultant   Winnipeg, Manitoba*
Heather Hayes   *Elementary Curriculum Consultant   City of Halifax Board of Education*
Gary Heck   *Curriculum Co-ordinator, Humanities   Lethbridge School District No. 51*
Ina Mary Rutherford   *Supervisor of Reading and Primary Instruction   Bruce County Board of Education*
Janice M. Sarkissian   *Supervisor of Instruction (Primary and Pre-School)   Greater Victoria School District*
Lynn Taylor   *Language Arts Consultant   Saskatoon Catholic School Board*

Acknowledgements
Very Tall Mouse and Very Short Mouse: Text and are of "VERY TALL MOUSE AND VERY SHORT MOUSE" from MOUSE TALES, written and illustrated by Arnold Lobel. Copyright © 1972 by Arnold Lobel. By permission of Harper & Row, Publishers, Inc. *Big and Little*: from LITTLE RACCOON AND POEMS FROM THE WOODS by Lilian Moore. Reprinted by permission of the publisher, McGraw-Hill Book Company, and Marian Reiner for the author. *Happiness*: From WHEN WE WERE VERY YOUNG by A. A. Milne. Copyright 1924 by E.P. Dutton, renewed 1952 by A. A. Milne. Reprinted by permission of The Canadian Publishers, McClelland and Stewart Limited, Toronto, and E.P. Dutton, a division of New American Library. *Where Have You Been?*: From WHERE HAVE YOU BEEN, text by Margaret Wise Brown, copyright ©. Permission by HASTINGS HOUSE, PUBLISHERS, INC. *The Friend*: Written and illustrated by John Burningham (Thomas Y. Crowell Co.) Copyright © 1975 by John Burningham. Reprinted by permission of Jonathan Cape Ltd. and Harper & Row, Publishers, Inc. *Making Valentines*: By J. Wolverton. Reprinted from AMERICAN SINGER. Copyright © 1961, American Book Co., by permission of D. C. Heath and Company. *One Bright Monday Morning*: From ONE BRIGHT MONDAY MORNING, by Arline and Joseph Baum. Copyright © 1962 by Arline Baum and Joseph Baum. Reprinted by permission of Random House, Inc. *Some Lollipops Last a Long, Long Time*: Reprinted by permission of Scholastic Inc. From THE LAUGH BOOK by Ruth Belov Gross. Copyright © 1971 by Ruth Belov Gross. *One Little Kitten*: Text and selected illustrations by Tana Hoban. Copyright © 1979 by Tana Hoban. By permission of Greenwillow Books (A Division of William Morrow & Co.). *Something Is There*: Lilian Moore, "Something Is There," in *See My Lovely Poison Ivy*. Copyright © 1975 Lilian Moore. Reprinted with the permission of Atheneum Publishers. *Do Little Chicks Pick Up Sticks?*: Excerpt from DO BABY BEARS SIT IN CHAIRS? by Ethel and Leonard Kessler. Copyright © 1961 by Ethel and Leonard Kessler. Reprinted by permission of Doubleday and Company, Inc. *Country Noisy Book*: Text excerpt from THE COUNTRY NOISY BOOK by Margaret Wise Brown. Copyright © 1940 by Margaret Wise Brown. Renewed 1968 by Roberta Brown Rauch. By permission of Harper & Row, Publishers, Inc. *Does a Goat Wear a Coat?*: By permission of Oak Tree Publications, Inc. Copyright © 1978 by Dr. Fitzhugh Dodson. From I WISH I HAD A COMPUTER THAT MAKES WAFFLES. . .by Dr. Fitzhugh Dodson. All rights reserved. *The Chicken and the Princes*: Excerpt form I'LL BE YOU AND YOU BE ME, written by Ruth Krauss, illustrated by Maurice Sendak. Text copyright © 1954 by Ruth Krauss. Pictures copyright © 1954 by Maurice Sendak. By permission of Harper & Row, Publishers, Inc.

Care has been taken to trace the ownership of copyright material used in this text. The publishers will welcome any information enabling them to rectify any reference or credit in subsequent editions.

Printed in Canada   11 12 13 14 15   99 98 97 96 95

Table of Contents

Very Tall Mouse and Very Short Mouse

by
Arnold Lobel

Once there was a very tall mouse
and a very short mouse
who were good friends.

When they met
Very Tall Mouse would say,
"Hello, Very Short Mouse."
And Very Short Mouse would say,
"Hello, Very Tall Mouse."

The two friends would often
take walks together.
As they walked along
Very Tall Mouse would say,
"Hello birds."
And Very Short Mouse would say,
"Hello bugs."

When they passed
by a garden
Very Tall Mouse would say,
"Hello flowers."
And Very Short Mouse would say,
"Hello roots."

When they passed by a house
Very Tall Mouse would say,
"Hello roof."
And Very Short Mouse
would say,
"Hello cellar."

One day the two mice
were caught in a storm.
Very Tall Mouse said,
"Hello raindrops."
And Very Short Mouse said,
"Hello puddles."

They ran indoors to get dry.
"Hello ceiling,"
said Very Tall Mouse.
"Hello floor,"
said Very Short Mouse.

Soon the storm was over.
The two friends ran
to the window.

Very Tall Mouse held
Very Short Mouse up to see.

"Hello rainbow!"
they both said together.

How Big Am I?

by
Wendy Cochran

I am big!

I am bigger than my baby brother.

I am bigger than
my best friend Anna.

I am bigger than
the twins next door.

I am not as big as a giraffe.
I am not as big as a hippopotamus.
I am not as big as a dinosaur.
NOBODY is that big!

Big and Little
by
Lilian Moore

Big is Me,
watching an ant
tug a dead bug
to a distant ant hill
blades of grass away.

Little is Me,
watching a bear
lift a paw
to scoop a bees' nest
from a tree.

15

Happiness

by
A. A. Milne

John had
Great Big Waterproof Boots on;
John had
a Great Big Waterproof Hat;
John had
a Great Big Waterproof Mackintosh—
And that
(said John) is that.

Where Have You Been?

by
Margaret Wise Brown

Little Old Cat
Little Old Cat
Where have you been?
To see this and that
Said the Little Old Cat
That's where I've been.

Little Old Squirrel
Little Old Squirrel
Where have you been?
I've been out on a whirl
Said the Little Old Squirrel
That's where I've been.

Little Old Fish
Little Old Fish
Where do you swim?
Wherever I wish
Said the Little Old Fish
That's where I swim.

Little Brown Bird
Little Brown Bird
Where do you fly?
I fly in the sky
Said the Little Brown Bird
That's where I fly.

Little Old Toad
Little Old Toad
Where have you been?
I've been way up the road
Said the Little Old Toad
That's where I've been.

Little Old Frog
Little Old Frog
Where have you been?
I've been sitting on a log
Said the Little Old Frog
That's where I've been.

Little Old Mole
Little Old Mole
Where have you been?
Down a long dark hole
Said the Little Old Mole
That's where I've been.

Little Old Bee
Little Old Bee
Where have you been?
In a pink apple tree
Said the Little Old Bee
That's where I've been.

Little Old Bunny
Little Old Bunny
Why do you run?
I run because it's fun
Said the Little Old Bunny
That's why I run.

Little Old Mouse
Little Old Mouse
Why run down the clock?
To see if the tick
Comes after the tock
I run down the clock.

Little Old Rook
Little Old Rook
Where do you look?
At the very last page
Of this very same book
Said the Little Old Rook.

Little Old Cat

Little Old Squirrel

Little Old Fish

Little Brown Bird

Little Old Toad

Little Old Frog

Little Old Mole

Little Old Bee

Little Old Bunny

Little Old Mouse

Little Old Rook

The Friend

by
John Burningham

Arthur is my friend.

We always
play together.

We play outside
when it is fine,

and stay inside
when it is raining.

Sometimes
I don't like Arthur.

So Arthur goes home.

Then I'm by myself.

I have other friends,
of course.

But Arthur is
my best friend.

A Goblin Lives in Our House
Traditional

A goblin lives in our house,
in our house, in our house,
A goblin lives in our house
all the year round.

He bumps
and he jumps
and he thumps
and he stumps.
He knocks
and he rocks
and he rattles at the locks.

A goblin lives in our house,
in our house, in our house,
A goblin lives in our house
all the year round.

Monkey Talk

by
David Booth

The Orangutan swings and climbs
through the forest trees.
He hoots and growls and roars.

The tiny Squirrel Monkey lives in the trees.
She can hang from a thin branch.
She eats fruit and insects.

The Gorilla looks like a gentle giant.
He beats his chest with his hands
when he is angry.

Chimpanzees are friendly apes.
They like to splash in the river.
They eat fruit, termites, and even pigs.

I Bought Me a Cat

by
Meguido Zola

I bought me a cat, my cat pleased me.
I fed my cat by the old elm tree.

My cat says, "Meow, meow."

I bought me a goose, my goose pleased me.
I fed my goose by the old elm tree.

My goose says, "Sss-sss."
My cat says, "Meow, meow."

I bought me a hen, my hen pleased me.
I fed my hen by the old elm tree.

My hen says, "Cluck, cluck."
My goose says, "Sss-sss."
My cat says, "Meow, meow."

I bought me a pig, my pig pleased me.
I fed my pig by the old elm tree.

My pig says, "Muck, muck."
My hen says, "Cluck, cluck."
My goose says, "Sss-sss."
My cat says, "Meow, meow."

I bought me a cow, my cow pleased me.
I fed my cow by the old elm tree.

My cow says, "Moo, moo."
My pig says, "Muck, muck."
My hen says, "Cluck, cluck."
My goose says, "Sss-sss."
My cat says, "Meow, meow."

I bought me a horse, my horse pleased me.
I fed my horse by the old elm tree.

My horse says, "Neigh, neigh."
My cow says, "Moo, moo."
My pig says, "Muck, muck."
My hen says, "Cluck, cluck."
My goose says, "Sss-sss."
My cat says, "Meow, meow."

I found me a friend, my friend pleased me.
I fed my friend by the old elm tree.
My friend says, "Hi there!"
My horse says, "Neigh, neigh."
My cow says, "Moo, moo."
My pig says, "Muck, muck."
My hen says, "Cluck, cluck."
My goose says, "Sss-sss."
My cat says, "Meow, meow."

Making Valentines

by
J. Wolverton

One red valentine,
Two red valentines,
Three red valentines,
Four.

I'll cut and cut,
and paste and paste,
and then make twenty more.

One Bright Monday Morning

by
Arline and Joseph Baum

One bright Monday morning
while on my way to school
   I saw...
1 blade of green grass growing
near a little blue pool.

One cool Tuesday morning
while on my way to school
   I saw...
2 blades of green grass growing,
1 pretty flower blooming
near a little blue pool.

One windy Wednesday morning
while on my way to school
   I saw...
3 blades of green grass growing,
2 pretty flowers blooming,
1 maple tree just budding
near a little blue pool.

58

One cloudy Thursday morning
while on my way to school
    I saw...
4 blades of green grass growing,
3 pretty flowers blooming,
2 maple trees just budding,
1 bird sweetly singing
near a little blue pool.

One rainy Friday morning
while on my way to school
    I saw...
5 blades of green grass growing,
4 pretty flowers blooming,
3 maple trees just budding,
2 birds sweetly singing,
1 bee busy buzzing
near a little blue pool.

One warm Saturday morning
in the park near my school
   I saw...
6 blades of green grass growing,
5 pretty flowers blooming,
4 maple trees just budding,
3 birds sweetly singing,
2 bees busy buzzing,
1 wiggle worm a-wiggling
near a little blue pool.

One sunny Sunday morning
in the park near my school
  I saw...
7 blades of green grass growing,
6 pretty flowers blooming,
5 maple trees just budding,
4 birds sweetly singing,
3 bees busy buzzing,
2 wiggle worms a-wiggling,
1 tiny ant a-crawling
near a little blue pool.

One bright Monday morning
while on my way to school
  I saw...
GRASS...growing!
FLOWERS...blooming!
TREES...budding!
BIRDS...singing!
BEES...buzzing!
WORMS...wiggling!
ANTS...crawling!

  It's SPRING!

Some Lollipops Last a Long, Long Time

by
Ruth Belov Gross

Some lollipops last a long, long time.
You lick and you lick and you lick,
and you keep on licking and licking
until all you have left to lick
is the empty lollipop stick.

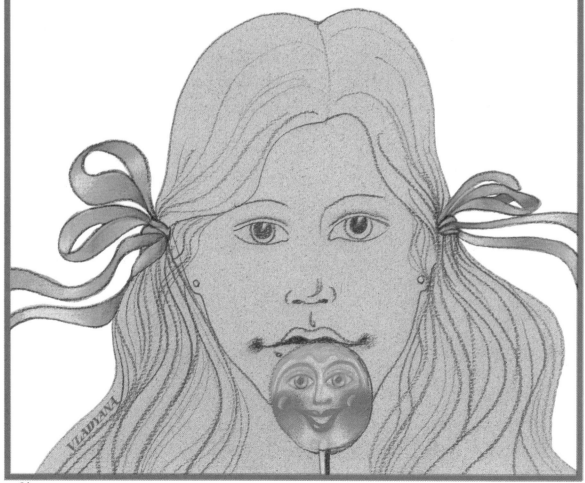

One Little Kitten

by
Tana Hoban

A new day!
It's time to play.

Just the thing—string!

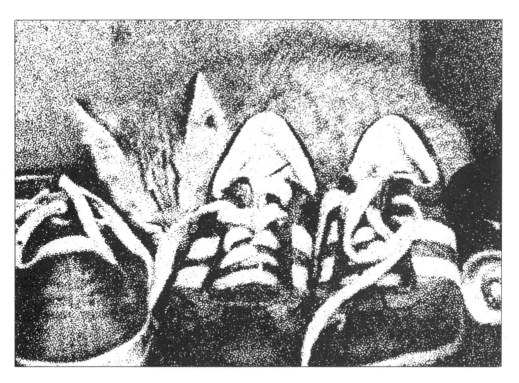

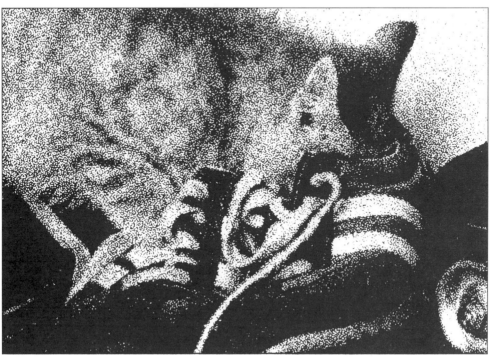

A funny place to put my face.

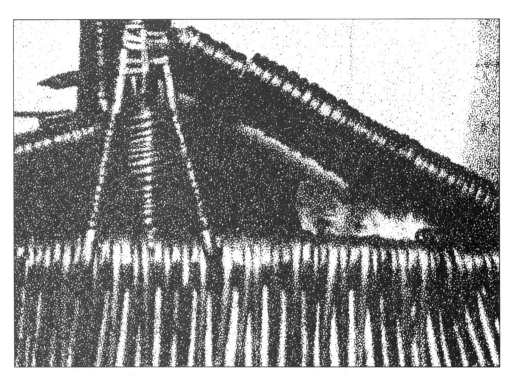

A place to hide inside.

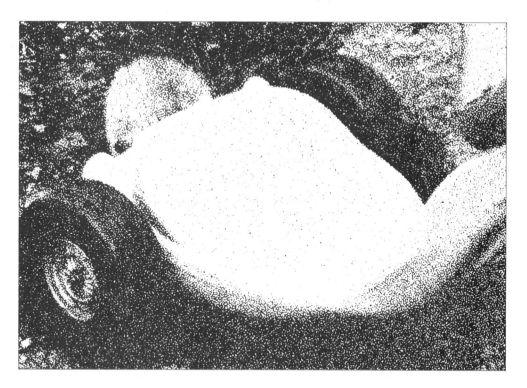

Where to? Through.

I'll disappear and come out here.

Is there room behind this broom?

It's getting late. Will they wait?

Hug me tight. Goodnight.

Something Is There

by
Lilian Moore

Something is there,
    there on the stair,
        coming down
            stepping with care.
        Coming down
            coming down
                slinkety-sly.
                    Something is coming
                        and wants to get by.

Do Little Chicks Pick Up Sticks?

by
Ethel and Leonard Kessler

Do little chicks
pick up sticks,

build with bricks,

play
funny
tricks?

No, no, no.
But they munch
on corn,
just as I do.

Do
buzzing
bees

swing in trees,

enjoy the breeze,

kick up their knees?
No...

But they smell the flowers,
just as I do!

Do baby bears,
or baby bees,
or little kittens
who climb up trees,
kangaroos or small raccoons,
or bugs or goats,
or seals or chicks,
get a goodnight
hug and kiss?

Oh, no!   But *I* do!

A Toad

by
Marla Stevenson

There once was a toad called Bufo,
who lived in a swamp in the middle of the bush
with mostly only other toads for company
and the odd frog.

Toads usually eat bugs,
if they eat at all,
as toads mainly sleep and hop around.

One day Bufo saw a marshmallow fall
white and soft beside a log.

He took a bite and liked it.
What a yummy treat for a toad!

Now, marshmallows are seldom seen
in the middle of the bush beside a swamp.

Bufo hasn't seen one since,
but he still remembers and waits and looks…
and in the meantime eats bugs.

Say Hello

by
David Booth

Say hello to creepy crawlers,
   Say hello to bees,
      Say hello to pussy willows,
        Hello there, if you please.

Say hello to early morning,
Say hello to noon,
Say hello to grass and sky,
Sing a hello tune.

Say hello to your best friend,
    Say hello to night,
        Say hello to slumber time,
            With the sheets tucked tight.

Say hello to daffodils,
Say hello to spring,
Say hello to whippoorwills,
Hello everything!

Country Noisy Book

by
Margaret Wise Brown

All around in the country it was dark,
and Muffin began to hear the night noises.

Whoo

Whooo

Whoo

Whooo

What was that?

Whippoorwill
Whippoorwill
Whippoorwill
      What was that?

Katydid
Katydidn't
Katydid
Katydidn't
      What was that?

Muffin walked past the pig pen.

Umph

Umph

Umph

What was that?

Eek

Eeeeek

Eeeeeek

What was that?

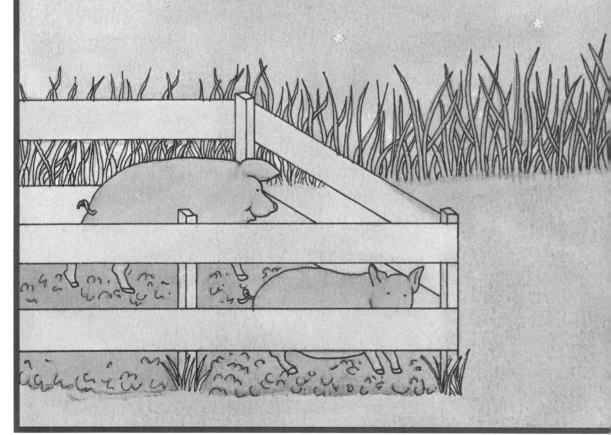

Then Muffin took a walk into the night,
and he walked past the frog pond.

Jugarum

Jugarum

Jugarum

What was that?

Flap
Flap
Flap

What was that?

Then a skunk went by without a sound.

All through the long grasses and in the trees
there were little lights flashing on and off,
little bug lights.

Wink
Wink
Wink

went the lightning bugs.
But could Muffin hear that?

Then Muffin was sleepy, so he went back into the house.
All was quiet except for a

tick tock tick tock
tick tock tick tock
cuckoo!
cuckoo!

Then he heard a soft
Prrrrrrrrrr
Prrrrrrrrrrrr
Prrrrrrrrrrrrrrrrrrrr.
What could that be?

It was a soft little pussycat,
warm and sleepy.
And Muffin curled up
with the soft little pussycat.

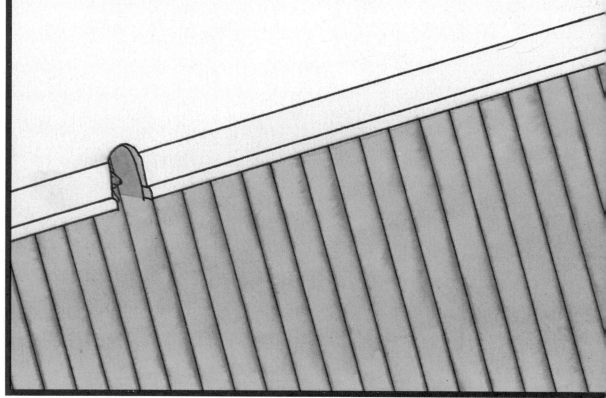

And then Muffin fell asleep and he didn't
hear any more noises.
Not even the wind.

Does a Goat Wear a Coat?

by
Dr. Fitzhugh Dodson

Does a goat wear a coat?

Can a mouse lift a house?

Can a cat fix a flat?

Can a duck drive a truck?

Can a kitten knit a mitten?

Can a hog learn to jog?

Does a snail get mail?

Department Store
by
Meguido Zola and David Booth

Monday's Cat

by
Meguido Zola and David Booth

Monday's cat is full of milk.
Tuesday's cat is smooth as silk.
Wednesday's cat will roam the house.
Thursday's cat can't catch his mouse.
Friday's cat licks clean her fur.
Saturday's cat just loves to purr.
Sunday's cat will scratch his head
and yawn and stretch
and stay in bed.

The Chicken and the Princess

by
Ruth Krauss and Maurice Sendak

One day the chicken

was going to town.

The chicken got lost.

But a princess found him.

She was nice.

And she was poor, the princess.

So he took her home to his house.